How CIOs Can Make Innovation Happen

Tips And Techniques For CIOs To Use In Order To Make Innovation Happen In Their IT Department

"Practical, proven techniques that will show you how to help your IT department to make innovation happen for them"

Dr. Jim Anderson

Published by:
Blue Elephant Consulting
Tampa, Florida

Copyright © 2013 by Dr. Jim Anderson

All rights reserved. No part of this book may be reproduced of transmitted in any form or by any means, electronic or mechanical, including photocopying, recording or by any information storage and retrieval system without written permission of the publisher, except for inclusion of brief quotations in a review.

Printed in the United States of America

Library of Congress Control Number: 2013922139

ISBN-13: 978-1494324018
ISBN-10: 1494324016

Warning – Disclaimer

The purpose of this book is to educate and entertain. This book does not promise or guarantee that anyone following the ideas, tips, suggestions, techniques or strategies will be successful. The author, publisher and distributor(s) shall have neither liability nor responsibility to anyone with respect to any loss or damage caused, or alleged to be caused, directly or indirectly by the information contained in this book.

Recent Books By The Author

Product Management

- How To Have A Successful Product Manager Career: The Things That You Need To Be Doing TODAY In Order To Have A Successful Product Manager Career

- Product Manager Product Success: How to keep your product on track and make it become a success

- Communication Skills For Product Managers: The Communication Skills That Product Managers Need To Know How To Use In Order To Have A Successful Product

- Customer Lessons For Product Managers: Techniques For Product Managers To Better Understand What Their Customers Really Want

Public Speaking

- Secrets To Planning The Perfect Speech

- Secrets To Organizing The Perfect Speech: How to organize the best speech of your life!

- Secrets To Creating The Perfect Speech: How to create a speech that will make your message be remembered forever!

- How To Rehearse In Order To Give The Perfect Speech: How to effectively rehearse your next speech to that your message be remembered forever!

CIO Skills

- CIO Business Skills: How CIOs can work effectively with the rest of the company!

- Managing Your CIO Career: Steps That CIOs Have To Take In Order To Have A Long And Successful Career

- CIO Communication Skills Secrets: Tips And Techniques For CIOs To Use In Order To Become Better Communicators

IT Manager Skills

- IT Manager Budgeting Skills

- IT Manager Career Secrets: Tips And Techniques That IT Managers Can Use In Order To Have A Successful Career

Negotiating

- Preparing For Your Next Negotiation: What You Need To Do BEFORE A Negotiation Starts In Order To Get The Best Possible Deal

- How To Open Your Next Negotiation: How To Start A Negotiation In Order To Get The Best Possible Outcome

Note: See a complete list of books by Dr. Jim Anderson at the back of this book.

Acknowledgements

Any book like this one is the result of years of real-world work experience. In my over 25 years of working for 7 different firms, I have met countless fantastic people and I've been mentored by some truly exceptional ones. Although I've probably forgotten some of the people who made me the person that I am today, here is my attempt to finally give them the recognition that they so truly deserve:

- Thomas P. Anderson
- Art Puett
- Bobbi Marshall
- Bob Boggs

Dr. Jim Anderson

This book is dedicated to my wife Lori. None of this would have been possible without her love and support.

Thanks for the best 21 years of my life (so far)...!

Table Of Contents

LIGHTING THE SPARK OF INNOVATION IS PART OF BEING A SUCCESSFUL CIO 8

ABOUT THE AUTHOR 10

CHAPTER 1: WHEN OPPORTUNITY COMES KNOCKING: GETTING REAL VALUE FROM ENTERPRISE SYSTEMS 15

CHAPTER 2: CREATIVE ABRASION: HOW TO BUILD INNOVATION INTO IT 18

CHAPTER 3: CAN HP SURVIVE? DO THEY HAVE THE SECRET CIO "JUICE"? 21

CHAPTER 4: FAUX MARKET SECRETS: HOW CIOS CAPTURE INNOVATION 25

CHAPTER 5: 4 INNOVATION STRATEGIES THAT ACTUALLY WORK 29

CHAPTER 6: CAN CIOS DRIVE INNOVATION & BOOST QUALITY AT THE SAME TIME? 34

CHAPTER 7: LAB RATS INVADE A CIO'S WORLD 38

CHAPTER 8: THE REASON THAT INNOVATION ISN'T HAPPENING IN YOUR IT DEPARTMENT 42

CHAPTER 9: CIOS ARE TRYING TO DO INNOVATION THE WRONG WAY 46

CHAPTER 10: 3 WAYS CIOS CAN SPARK INNOVATION IN THEIR IT DEPARTMENTS 50

CHAPTER 11: 3 STEPS CIOS CAN TAKE TO MAKE INNOVATION HAPPEN FOR THEIR IT DEPARTMENT 54

CHAPTER 12: CIO'S KNOW THAT FINDING THE RIGHT WAY TO BE INNOVATIVE IS THE HARD PART 58

Lighting The Spark Of Innovation Is Part Of Being A Successful CIO

Every company wants to grow and become more successful. There is no magic formula to make this happen, but it is generally agreed that in order for this to happen the company cannot stand still. Instead, they always have to be trying new things and growing.

In the IT department, in order to make this kind of growth occur, innovation has to be encouraged to happen. All too often the workers in the IT department can get too involved in their day-to-day tasks to spend any time thinking about innovation. That's where the CIO has to step in.

As the CIO it is your job to create an IT environment in your department that will not only encourage innovation to happen but will also help it to grow once it starts. A great deal of this has to do with how you communicate to the rest of the department what you want to happen.

Innovation is something that we all know that we want to have happen, but just exactly how to make it occur is what often eludes us. As CIO you are going to have to identify the innovation strategies that will work with your company and your department and then implement them.

It's possible that either innovation projects have been tried in the past and have not worked or, more likely, there is no innovation going on right now. It is your job to change this and make innovation take root and become part of everyone's daily routine.

This book is filled with tools that CIOs can use to introduce innovation into their IT departments. These ideas range from using creative abrasion to employing faux market secrets. No matter what approach you decide to take, the goal is the same: cause innovation to take root and grow.

Making innovation happen is not easy. By reading this book you will have the ideas and the techniques that you need to cause it to happen in your IT department. Once this happens, it can spread to the rest of the company. This is the kind of leadership that the company is looking for from their IT department.

For more information on what it takes to be a great CIO, check out my blog, The Accidental Successful CIO, at:

www.TheAccidentalSuccessfulCIO.com

Good luck!

- Dr. Jim Anderson

About The Author

I must confess that I never set out to be a CIO. When I went to school, I studied Computer Science and thought that I'd get a nice job programming and that would be that. Well, at least part of that plan worked out!

My first job was working for Boeing on their F/A-18 fighter jet program. I spent my days programming fighter jet software in assembly language and I loved it. The U.S. government decided to save some money and went looking for other countries to sell this plane to. This put me into an unfamiliar role: I started to meet with foreign military officials and I ended up having to manage groups of engineers who were working on international projects.

Time moved on and so did I. I found myself working for Siemens, the big German telecommunications company. They were making phone switches and selling them to the seven U.S. phone companies. The problem was that the switches were too complicated. Customers couldn't tell the difference between one complicated phone switch from another complicated phone switch. Once again I found myself working with the sales and marketing teams to find ways to make the great technology that the engineers had developed understandable to both internal and external customers.

I've spent over 25 years working as an senior IT professional for both big companies and startups. This has given me an opportunity to learn what it takes to manage and IT department in ways that allow it to maximize its output while becoming a valuable part of the overall company.

I now live in Tampa Florida where I spend my time managing my consulting business, Blue Elephant Consulting, teaching college courses at the University of South Florida, and traveling to work with companies like yours to share the knowledge that I have about how to create and manage successful IT departments.

I'm always available to answer questions and I can be reached at:

Dr. Jim Anderson
Blue Elephant Consulting
Email: jim@BlueElephantConsulting.com
Facebook: http://goo.gl/1TVoK
Web: http://www.BlueElephantConsulting.com/

"Unforgettable communication skills that will set your ideas free…"

Create IT Departments That Are Productive And A Valuable Asset To The Rest Of The Company !

Dr. Jim Anderson is available to provide training and coaching on the topics that are the most important to people who have to manage IT departments: how can I build a productive IT department (and keep it together) while at the same time providing the rest of the company with the IT services that they need?

Dr. Anderson believes that in order to both learn and remember what he says, speakers need to laugh. Each one of his speeches is full of fun and humor so that what he says "sticks" with everyone.

Dr. Anderson's CIO SkillsTraining Includes:

1. How to identify and attract the right type of IT workers to your IT department.
2. How to build relationships with the company's senior management in order to get the support that you need?
3. How to stay on top of changing technology and security issues so that you never get surprised?

Dr. Jim Anderson works with over 100 customers per year. To invite Dr. Anderson to work with you, contact him at:

Phone: 813-418-6970 or
Email: jim@BlueElephantConsulting.com

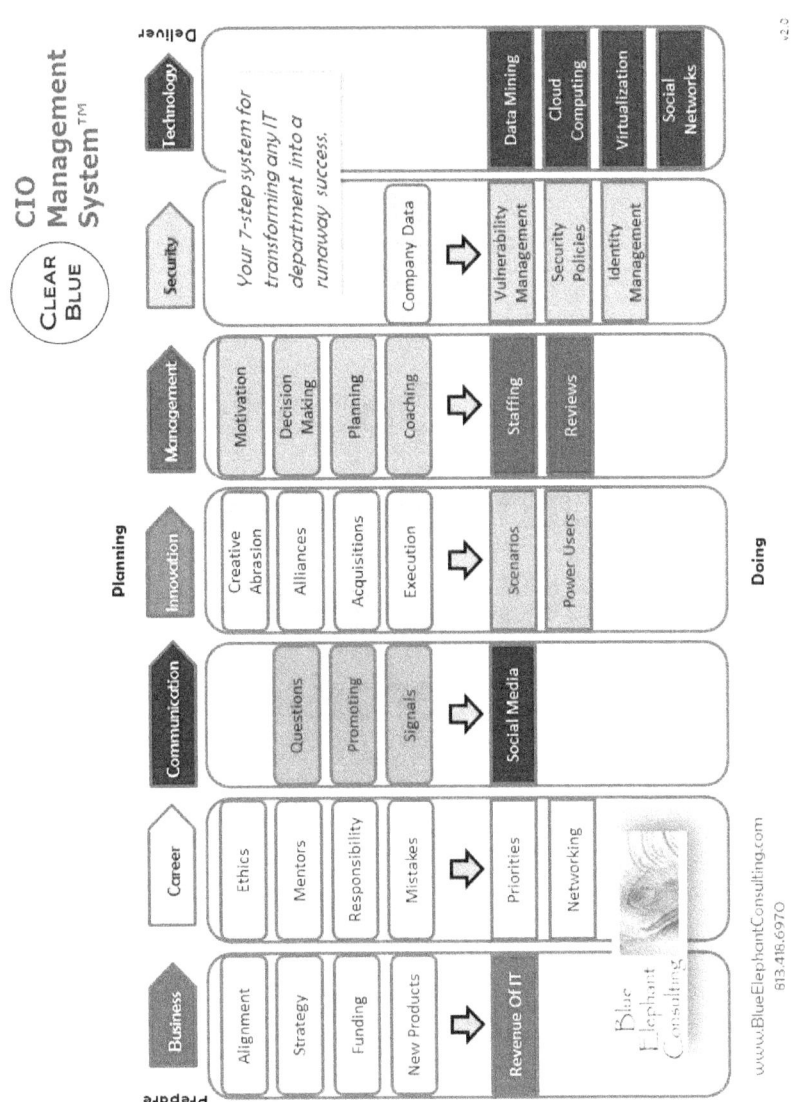

The Clear Blue CIO Management System™ has been created to provide CIOs and senior IT managers with a clear roadmap for how to manage an IT department. This system shows CIOs what needs to be done and in what order to do it.

Chapter 1

When Opportunity Comes Knocking: Getting Real Value From Enterprise Systems

Chapter 1: When Opportunity Comes Knocking: Getting Real Value From Enterprise Systems

The good folks over at Accenture have started running some ads that are asking companies to take a long term look at the value of those really big IT projects such as CRM systems and other enterprise systems. They make a really good point that lots of companies are doing the work, but missing the point. To quote from their ad:

Companies often neglect to factor in business strategy when putting an enterprise system in place, says Kevin Carnahan, managing director of system integration for Accenture in San Francisco.

Often companies err by focusing on getting software installed, but they miss the opportunity to get the analytics and the forward-looking information enterprise systems can provide, he adds.

"They may get systems working in a way that keeps the business operating. That has a fundamental value, but companies need to take the extra step to transform transaction-level data into action-oriented metrics that enable management decisions."

Elsewhere in the ad/article, they point out that the Accenture Institute for High Performance Business conducted two studies, four years apart, to examine the practices that enable companies to get more value out of their investments in enterprise systems.

The studies consistently showed that senior executives' top priority for their systems is to obtain better information for decision making. Hmm, this sounds like a job for the CIO and the IT team!

Having lived through several implementations of these types of systems, I can attest to the fact that just getting them in place and working is a bear of a task. Most of the firms that I've worked for have been so exhausted by the process that they have pretty much stopped here.

After all, there really aren't a lot of stories about companies that have leveraged their enterprise systems to become more competitive. Just lots of disaster stories about when implementation projects go off track.

As CIOs and IT departments strive to find new roles to replace the operations ones that are going away, it sure looks like using the enterprise systems to answer questions for the rest of the business is a great way to show value for the department.

How would one actually go about doing this? Well basically we are talking about collecting copious amounts of data and then further processing it in order to detect trends and spot abnormalities.

The collection and processing tasks are well suited to the IT shop. There's a good chance that the data will have to be cleaned and the output of the processing will have to be analyzed in order to ensure that you are not getting good looking garbage numbers.

Both of these tasks are not well suited for any other part of the company to perform. It will require a reorganization of the IT department and a retraining of the CIO so that he/she can present the results of the analysis in a way that matches how the business teams see the world.

Additionally, the CIO will be part of a feedback loop that brings requests for further analysis back to the IT team. Welcome to a brave new world — that's opportunity that you hear knocking!

Chapter 2

Creative Abrasion: How To Build Innovation Into IT

Chapter 2: Creative Abrasion: How To Build Innovation Into IT

While trolling the Internet over the holidays, I came across a write-up of the Unstructure Event held that was held Orlando, Florida, USA during November of 2008.

Unstructure is basically a platform for open discussions on a wide range of business topics. They had a face-to-face meeting back in November. What caught my eye is that they spent some time discussing one of my favorite topics, IT and business innovation.

If you need a great quote on how IT leaders need to behave, you can always count on Nelson Mandela:

"A leader... is like a shepherd. He stays behind the flock, letting the most nimble go on ahead, whereupon the others follow, not realizing that all along they are being directed from behind" – Nelson Mandela.

During the Unstructure conference, Linda Hill from the Harvard Business School, ran a panel that included four panelists from companies such as Cisco, Powerwave, Smiths Medical and another teacher from Carnegie Mellon.

The panel's primary focus was on trying to answer the question "How can an IT department unlock innovation within the organization?"

Sure, a manager can tell / force the people who work for him/her to do things and that will cause things to occur. However, a true leader can create a world that people want to belong to. He or she can harness talent and bring together diverse slices of the genius of the people in the department who need to affirm individual identity and allow them to contribute to the larger goal. That's the difference between a manager and a leader.

I think that Linda Hill hit it on the head when she said that: *There is a need for collective work through creative abrasion, creative agility, integrative problem solving, a sense of belonging and civic engagement. Amplify differences and leverage them as resources even though it does not feel good. A person needs to feel a part of a community to want to give them his/her slice of genius, else it makes them feel vulnerable.*

Linda also said that: Innovation happens when artistry blends with Engineering. It takes both sides of the mind, and different disciplines or specialists working together to breed innovation. When Imagination meets Engineering Precision, this makes for a positive impact and changes the way the world lives, works, plays and learns.

From an IT point-of-view, the question is will technology play a role? We all know that the answer is yes! The next wave of innovation will be captured through collaboration and connecting ideas from both inside and outside of the IT department.

As much as we'd all like to have our IT departments be known as being innovative, the question remains: how? Speakers on the Unstructure panel said that innovation cannot be nurtured in a streamlined process. An example of this was the campaign run by Barack Obama in the elections where several new channels were used to run the campaign.

Good discussions all around – my hat is off to the folks over at Unstructure. It appears as though it's still not clear how we can transform an IT department into a smooth running innovation machine. However, we seem to be asking the right questions and we are making progress in working towards finding an answer that will work for us all.

Chapter 3

Can HP Survive? Do They Have The Secret CIO "Juice"?

Chapter 3: Can HP Survive? Do They Have The Secret CIO "Juice"?

HP's CIO Randy Mott has done some fantastic things in helping to turn the company around. However, now things are starting to get tricky and it's not clear that the company is going to be able to continue to be successful. Everyone seems to think that what they need is a shot of that "**innovation juice**" and it's not clear that Randy's going to be able to deliver it...

What HP Did Right

Ok, so let's admit it – HP had lost their way under Carly Fiorina's guidance. They brought in Mark Hurd as CEO (who then brought in Randy Mott as CIO) to turn things around. Hat's off to Mark – he's done **a great job**.

Ashlee Vance over at the New York Times had a chance to talk with Hurd awhile back and he revealed that he sees HP in terms of four "**quadrants**". These quadrants include operations, products, business & technology trends, and competitors.

Clearly Hurd has an analytical outlook on life – many people have remarked on just how good he is with balance sheets and dealing with numbers in general. It turns out that this is both **good and bad**.

The Problem That HP Has Now

HP has done a fantastic job of cutting staff, reducing costs, and negotiating great deals on parts. Having achieved just about all of the benefits that one can get from doing these types of actions, the question that comes up is "**what next**?"

Shareholders like growth and in the immediate past, HP's been growing by cutting. Now that that's all done, how will it maintain its growth? This is where that pesky thing called **innovation** comes in...

Old Solutions Won't Work!

HP used to be able to count on the famous **HP labs** to come up with new product ideas that would show them the way forward. However, in the current era of budget cutting and project justifications, HP has shrunk the number of projects that their labs are working on from 130 down to about 50. That may not be enough to have enough of those "eureka" moments where breakthroughs happen.

Next Steps For HP

The trick here is to find a way to recapture that "juice" that a technology company like HP needs to have in order to survive. This is exactly where **CIO Randy Mott** should step in.

As CIO of HP, Randy is in a unique position to help Hurd out. Since HP sells information technology products and services, their very own CIO is the person who can help them **evaluate which ideas they need to run with**.

Yes, yes – both Hurd and Mott like to run a tight ship with metrics ruling the day. I believe that that time has come and (partially) gone. Now is the time for Mott to **throw open the doors** to his IT department and start up some trial projects and initiatives. HP is so large that they could easily run multiple evaluations in parallel.

Final Thoughts

HP has made a remarkable comeback from the brink of despair. However, as they try to move forward, innovation and clever sparks of imagination are what's going to be needed. HP's CIO Randy Mott has the resources and the talent in his shop that would allow HP to use itself as a testing ground for **encouraging its employees to make suggestions** and have them tried out. Let's see if they make the most of this opportunity...

Chapter 4

Faux Market Secrets: How CIOs Capture Innovation

Chapter 4: Faux Market Secrets: How CIOs Capture Innovation

So picture this: you're a CIO and you desperately want to be seen by the rest of the C-level executives as something more than a simple cost center. What to do? If only there was some way that you could tap into all of that incredible **creative energy** that we all know lives in the IT department.

If you could harness that energy and apply it to innovative projects, you'd be a company hero. Guess what? The power of **Faux Markets** is exactly what you need to do this…

What Is A Faux Market?

You know that things are getting fancy when we start using French words! A Faux Market is simply a term that refers to using **simulated market forces** to make a decision. Perhaps an example would show what I mean. A good case study would be GE Research.

Back in 2005 GE Research had a problem. They had too many product ideas that had been submitted and only $50,000 to spend on investigating them. Clearly they need to make some **hard decisions** as to which ones they would pursue.

The way they picked which projects to work on was by using a faux market. They had their 85 employees spend three weeks buying and selling any one of 62 proposed projects. At the end of the three weeks, GE ended up with a **prioritized list of the top projects** that its employees thought had the most value. The project that won was a machine intelligence algorithm that a researcher had proposed but which had not yet traveled through the normal management bureaucracy.

Why Use Faux Markets?

All too often IT departments have a bewildering array of possible projects, technologies, or directions that the department can choose. Sometimes senior management will huddle and make a decision, sometimes no decision gets made. **Faux markets offer an alternative.**

A faux market tool allows a firm to quickly sort through large numbers of projects or proposals in order to attempt find those that will provide the most bang for the buck. Firms believe that this approach offers them the best chance of finding the next **blockbuster product** or solution.

Not A Silver Bullet

Faux markets can be a big help; however, as with everything else they do have their drawbacks. One such drawback is that the voting process does not provide much **insight** - there may be no penalty for backing a bad idea. Just because a proposal is popular does not necessarily guarantee commercial success.

Final Thoughts

Using faux market tools to quickly sort through a large stack of ideas can provide IT departments with a way to identify innovative ideas no matter where they come from. However, a group vote alone **isn't enough** in most cases.

A two-step process where voting is initially used to narrow a large list down into a more manageable list of less than 100 candidates is a good first step. The next step can be to use a **prediction market** which allows employees to buy and sell the candidates in order to see which ones go up in value. This will reveal the true winning ideas and you will have **found a way** to apply IT to enable the rest of the company to grow quicker, move faster, and do more.

Chapter 5

4 Innovation Strategies That Actually Work

Chapter 5: 4 Innovation Strategies That Actually Work

Innovation, innovation, innovation – everyone wants it, but nobody seems know how to get and keep it. CIOs are under a lot of pressure to do more with less these days and being able to nurture an environment of innovation sure would help. The trick is knowing HOW to do this...

The Problem With Innovation

One of the big problems that CIOs have is that when they start to think about innovation, they start by imagining a big blank sheet of paper and then they try to figure out how they can be innovative. This is exactly the wrong approach.

It turns out that how to innovate is NOT a blank sheet of paper – what techniques work is well known and now what techniques work together is also known. Two professors, Dr Frank Rothaermel and Dr. Edward Hess have taken a close look at what innovation techniques work, and they've discovered **the four that work best**.

Four Types Of Innovation

The first thing that CIOs need to realize is that there is no **one-size-fits-all** solution to finding an innovation strategy that works for a firm. Instead, there are four different approaches that seem to work the best. Just to make things more complicated, each of the four different approaches can be combined. However, not all combinations result in more innovation. Let's take a closer look.

The four different types of innovation that work best for firms are:

- Recruiting & cultivating human capital,
- Spending more on internal R&D
- Strategic alliances,
- Acquiring technology ventures

It is important to note that all four approaches can be pursued individually or all at once. However, going after more than one approach can allow a firm to achieve a higher level of innovation, but some strategies don't mix well and can cause a firm to end up wasting both time and money. The key is to know which techniques work well **with each other**.

The Best Way To Foster Innovation

You knew that I was going to say this: the research shows that the best way to achieve continuous innovation over time is to **hire and cultivate talented people**. As always, this is something that is easy to say, but very hard to do.

The reason that taking the time and investing the money in your staff is the best way to foster long term innovation is because this approach allows an IT department to have **more control** over their IP and creates a **steadier pipeline** of innovation since no outside partners are being relied on.

To improve the odds of this approach working, the best IT departments build teams that are made up of both **star and non-star employees**. This allows the stars to look for new ideas while the non-stars turn ideas into successful products. Once again, you can see that although this is a powerful idea, it takes some serious CIO management skills to make it happen.

How To Combine Innovation Techniques

When a CIO decides that innovation must be boosted, all too often they will start throwing money at a variety of different techniques without fully understanding how they will (or won't) **work together.**

For example, investing money in creating **alliances** is often done to create the same type of knowledge that companies can get from investing in their own people.

CIOs that invest in both approaches end up wasting money because of the **overlap**. The key question that a CIO needs to answer before perusing an alliance on top of developing star and non-star employees is to understand what **key assets will be gained** through the alliance that he/she can't get from their own employees.

Dr. Rothaermel and Dr. Hess have discovered that the two approaches that **work the best together** are alliances and acquisitions. CIOs that take the time to form a joint venture with a vendor partner company before trying to buy it gives the CIO critical inside information on the target firm.

It turns out that both alliances and internal R&D spending also **complement each other**. Internally developed knowledge allows CIOs to better understand what market areas will become promising and this allows them to invest in the most promising alliances.

Final Thoughts

There is saying that goes "there is nothing new under the sun." This holds true for CIOs that are seeking to boost the innovation in their departments.

It turns out that studies have shown that there are **four innovation techniques** that work the best. These four techniques can be combined and used together; however, CIOs should only pursue multiple innovation strategies if they complement each other. CIOs who can grow innovation within their departments will have **found a way** to apply IT to enable the rest of the company to grow quicker, move faster, and do more.

Chapter 6

Can CIOs Drive Innovation & Boost Quality At The Same Time?

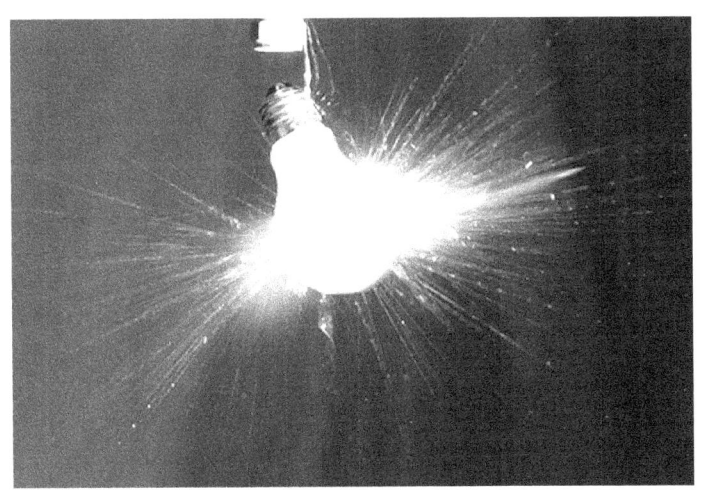

Chapter 6: Can CIOs Drive Innovation & Boost Quality At The Same Time?

How are you at walking and chewing gum at the same time? It's sorta a classic challenge – do two different things simultaneously and **do them well**. CIOs are facing the challenge today – cut costs and simultaneously use IT to make the business more competitive. How hard can that be?

Say Hello To Six Sigma

If you've been to a book store recently and looked at any of the books in the business section, you may have been overwhelmed by the number of titles that had the words "**Six Sigma**" in them. Six Sigma is an approach to business that makes use of constant measurement and analysis in order to continue to optimize business operations.

Dr. Sara Beckman has researched this technique and points out that Six Sigma was invented at Motorola and popularized by Jack Welch at GE. If you apply it to how an IT shop goes about doing its work, it can be a great way to **drive out costs and boost quality**. However, it will do nothing to drive innovation.

Say Hello To Design Thinking

Design thinking is a new set of skills that are designed to drive innovative thinking. The starting point for design thinking is for solution designers (who else?) to start by focusing on what **problems** their customers are having on a daily basis. Once they understand the problems, the next step is to consider the wide universe of possible ways to solve these problems.

The Problem

Here in lies the problem. If you go out and talk to today's CIOs you'll find that they have generally implemented **one** of these two different solutions (Six Sigma is more popular because it's easier to understand and measure).

This causes problems. It is possible to **focus too much** on driving out costs and then lose your way and not be able to provide the innovation in IT that is needed to keep the business competitive – this is the problem that HP is currently facing.

Likewise, if an IT department is **too innovative** and doesn't watch the bottom line closely enough, then they can quickly drive themselves and the company out of business. The dot.com fiasco was a great example of this.

What's The Correct Solution To This Problem?

You may have already guessed it, but the right way to solve this challenge is for CIOs to take the time to find a way to **incorporate both** the design thinking and the Six Sigma approaches into their IT departments.

The design thinking technique allows an IT department to find ways to explore **new approaches** to solving the problems that the business is facing. Six Sigma techniques allow an IT department to find ways to **improve** how they are currently doing things.

Final Thoughts

CIOs can't allow their IT departments to become too focused on just one approach or they **risk failing**. Design thinking tries to find out what a good solution to a problem is while Six Sigma assumes that a solution is good and then goes about trying to make it even better.

CIOs who can find a way to reduce costs while at the same time driving IT innovation will be better at finding ways to apply IT to enable the rest of the company to **grow quicker, move faster, and do more**.

Chapter 7

Lab Rats Invade A CIO's World

Chapter 7: Lab Rats Invade A CIO's World

I work in the telecommunications field a lot and the **gold standard** of corporate R&D labs has always been Bell Labs. These guys have created amazing things that we all take for granted today: transistors, fiber optics, etc.

Since most firms have no idea about what to do with their corporate research facilities, responsibility for the labs often falls **under the control of the CIO** (because most firms don't know what to do with IT either). Great. So what's a CIO to do when he/she is responsible for a corporate R&D lab?

The Times They Are A Changing

So why did companies set up their research labs in the first place? Simple, they needed **a source of innovation** that they could harness in order to become more successful. Unfortunately, the Internet came along and the wheels have fallen off this truck.

In the old days (the early 90's), researchers used **social networks** to exchange information and drive their research forward. No, not Facebook or Twitter – we're talking about the early 90's here. They used the REAL social networks that formed when researchers went to conferences or met in the lunchroom.

The arrival of the Internet has turned this world **upside down**. If you can connect with anyone over the Internet, then why would you even bother to have a corporate R&D lab?

It turns out that there is still a reason for corporate R&D lab, it's just that they are going to be **much smaller** and the value of even having an R&D lab will go down.

CIO's And The New Era Of R&D

Steve Lohr over at the New York Times has been talking with folks in the corporate R&D world to find out what **the future of R&D Labs** is going to look like.

Pull the cover off an R&D lab and you'll discover **a machine** that can turn ideas into products. In the future, the ideas that a business can turn into a product (which is what a business is in business to do) won't come from a lab, instead they will be coming from all over. Wow, what a mess.

In the future companies aren't going to be able to afford to have the old style R&D labs. These labs were paid for by corporate profits. Once again, that dang Internet thing has come along and **leveled the playing field** and those corporate profits are now under pressure from everywhere. Now that they are gone, there's no way to pay for old-style R&D.

The new way (practiced by HP, GE, and IBM) is for CIOs to transform what a corporate R&D lab does. The new role for an R&D lab is for it to act as a **communications hub** between researchers who can all be located at remote locations.

The sources of new ideas can be universities, start-ups, other businesses, and even government labs. Researchers will have to start acting like **human Googles** and start sucking up all of the information that they need to create products that their firms can sell.

Final Thoughts

CIOs who find themselves in charge of a company's R&D labs have a delicate challenge on their hands. No matter how successful the labs have been in the past, the past is the past and what worked then **will no longer work**. CIOs need to move aggressively to transform how R&D research is done.

Realizing the Internet changes everything, CIOs will have to create an R&D "**hub and spoke**" logical design where the corporate R&D team funnels communications between multiple parties in order to move innovation along. Ultimately, when enough information has been gathered to allow a product to be created, then a CIO will know that his / her R&D lab is doing what it needs to do.

Chapter 8

The Reason That Innovation Isn't Happening In Your IT Department

Chapter 8: The Reason That Innovation Isn't Happening In Your IT Department

How many times do you have to tell your IT department: it's time to start innovating again? The global recession is over, if your company is going to start to grow and be successful, then the IT department is going to have to be out in front and leading the charge. Since budgets are still constrained, it's going to take a great deal of innovation to find ways to do more with what you currently have. Why isn't anyone doing this?

You Are Not Alone

I'm not sure if this is going to make you feel any better, but as CIO (or as almost-CIO) you are not alone in this absence of innovation. Lots of firms are finding that their IT departments are missing that spark of innovation also.

What's going on here? That's the very question that two researchers, Feirong Yuan and Richard Woodman , set out to answer. They sent out surveys to 100's of employees of companies and they covered everyone from the top of the pyramid to the folks working in the mailroom.

It's All About Image

Their findings were actually quite interesting. What they discovered is that innovation in an IT department is being withheld because IT staff are concerned about the risk to their workplace image that being seen as being innovative would cause. The power of creating unfavorable social impressions with their coworkers is what is keeping their mouths shut.

A lot of this can be tied back to just exactly what a given IT worker's job title is. If it doesn't explicitly say "innovator" in their job description, then you've got a problem. IT workers who are not expected to be innovators feel that their coworkers will develop a negative impression of them if they start to suggest different ways of doing things.

This goes even one step further. The researchers discovered that many IT employees fear that too much innovation on their part will start to "provoke anger" among their fellow IT coworkers. This will be especially true with those workers who are happy with the way that things are – the "don't rock the boat" mentality.

The Role Of The CIO

As the CIO, it's going to be your job to make innovation happen in your IT department. If you don't, then you won't be CIO for very long. What you are going to have to communicate to the entire IT department is that the whole organization is behind the push for more innovation.

Showing that innovation is what is being expected will go a long way in setting the stage for your IT staff. Telling the department over and over again that you are looking for them to be innovative will serve to lower the perceived social risk of coming forward with innovative suggestions.

Your job as CIO is to create an IT workplace where your staff will feel comfortable in being innovative. This means that you are going to have to make everyone understand that individual differences are not only tolerated, but are actually critical in order to help the IT department look at problems in different ways.

What All Of This Means For You

As CIO you are going to have to make the most out of the resources that you have – funding will always be tight. This means that you are going to have to find ways to get your IT department's staff to get creative and innovate. However, recent studies have shown that workers who are not expected to be innovative often worry about their image and don't speak up.

In order to change this, as CIO you are going to have to clearly and repeatedly communicate to the IT department that innovation is not only encouraged, but it is also expected. You're going to have to create an environment in which all workers feel comfortable speaking up and being innovative.

There is no one magic action that you can take to make your IT department be more innovative. However, given time and a consistent message from you that innovation is a good thing, you can convince everyone in your IT department to think hard and become the innovation engine that the company is going to need in order to both survive and thrive.

Chapter 9

CIOs Are Trying To Do Innovation The Wrong Way

Chapter 9: CIOs Are Trying To Do Innovation The Wrong Way

As the world slowly recovers from its great economic recession, CIOs are gearing up to help their companies do battle with their competitors. Everywhere in this great land you can hear the same words being repeated **"I want more innovation!"** Umm, ok. It turns out that innovation doesn't just happen. Instead you need a whole bunch of little changes first. Maybe I should explain...

Innovation Requires Many Little Changes

All too often CIOs believe that their staff just needs to spend more time sitting around thinking in order to have more of those **"big bang" moments** where innovative thoughts just jump in to their heads. Sadly, it turns out that things just don't seem to work out this way.

Dr. Rosabeth Kanter has been studying how innovation works in companies and she's discovered something that I think that we've all suspected for some time. It turns out in order to make the big innovative changes, company's first need to make a whole series of **smaller incremental changes**.

What Dr. Kanter has found is that those really big ideas that we all like to spend so much time talking about are really **the result of a lot of other work**. It's the incremental changes that were put into place to change how we deal with partners or how we distribute our information that allows a CIO's team to come up with the big innovation.

It's All About The Pyramid

Dr. Kanter suggests that that we view innovation not as a stand-alone item, but rather as **a pyramid**. This pyramid consists of three different, but related, levels.

The broad base of the pyramid is made up of all of the incremental changes that need to be made in order to set the stage for greater things. Making these changes increases an IT department's **level of operational excellence**.

The middle layer of the pyramid is **the idea factory** – this is where new and novel ideas are allowed to hatch and grow. An IT department needs to be able to allow such ideas to flourish and provide them with the resources that they need in order to grow.

Finally, at the top of the innovation pyramid are those few innovative ideas that appear to have the ability to **significantly change the company**. These are the ideas that need to get the IT department's full backing and access to the additional resources and talent that will be required in order to allow them to truly transform the company.

What All Of This Means For You

Yes, IT innovation is great stuff – that's where things like the iPhone and the Kindle came from. However, CIOs who walk around telling their teams to be more innovative are **missing the point**.

It turns out that in order for innovation to happen, firms have to first take the time to make lots and lots of **smaller changes**. You need to effectively set the stage for your innovation to happen. By doing this a CIO can create an environment in which the innovation that he or she is looking for will occur.

The **"pyramid of innovation"** shows that you can't just get innovation by itself. Instead you need to get a combination package of incremental improvements and that will in turn allow innovation to happen. CIOs who master this will find that perhaps getting innovation out of their IT department is not so hard after all...

Chapter 10

3 Ways CIOs Can Spark Innovation In Their IT Departments

Chapter 10: 3 Ways CIOs Can Spark Innovation In Their IT Departments

If Steve Jobs was still with us, do you think that he might be willing to come and work in your IT department? He was supposed to be a jerk, but man can he **bring some innovation to the table**. CIOs who want to foster more innovation in their IT departments probably couldn't get Steve to sign up with their IT team; however, I've got three suggestions that just might light the spark of innovation within your IT department.

Ask And You Shall Receive

So why isn't there more innovation going on in your IT department? Based on how much time CIOs spend talking about innovation; you'd almost think that it was a part of the definition of information technology. One reason that innovation isn't happening is because **you may be looking for it in the wrong places**. The companies in the IT sector that are the most innovative know that the best ideas can come from anywhere in the organization.

The problem is that all too often IT employees feel that they have **too little opportunity to provide input** to improve the way that things are being done. Confirmation of this has been revealed by studies that show that the average U.S. employee's ideas are implemented once every six years! It should be pretty obvious that innovative companies are the ones who spend more time implementing more of their employee's ideas.

As CIO you need to clearly communicate to everyone in the IT department that **you value their ideas** and that you want them to suggest them. You'll have to take the extra step and show them that their ideas are being implemented in order to get them to make more suggestions.

You Gotta Make Time

Just exactly **when do you think that your IT staff will be coming up with these innovative ideas?** If they are working non-stop from the moment that they arrive at work until the time that they leave, you won't be getting the innovative ideas from them that your IT department so desperately needs.

This is exactly the kind of issue that only a CIO can step in and solve. You are going to have to very clearly communicate **just how important you view innovation as being**. After you do that, you're going to have to put your money where your mouth is.

As CIO you are going to have to **carve out time** during the work week that your IT department employees can use to work on creative ideas. Clearly not all of these ideas are going to result in something that will benefit the company. However, the bet is that enough of them will so that it will make it all worthwhile.

It's All About Execution

As CIO you might think that the most difficult part of the innovation process is coming up with the new idea. You'd be wrong. It turns out that where we all seem to struggle the most is in **executing the ideas**. Once again, this is where the CIO can step in and make things happen.

As CIO you need to **establish a clear process** that the IT department can use in order to prioritize ideas that IT staff are creating, assign resources to the most promising new ideas, and then find ways to test the ideas.

Finding ways to do all of these steps **quickly and cheaply** means that your IT department will be able to run more experiments and that means that you'll be able to reject the ideas that don't pan out and keep the ones that provide the greatest benefits.

What All Of This Means For You

We all like to talk about the importance of information technology, but in reality, innovation is the thing that allows an IT department to continue to improve. A part of every CIOs job is to find ways that will allow his or her IT department **to do a better job of innovating more**.

It's not easy to do all of the things that an IT department has to do and be innovative. This is where the CIO comes in. You are going to need to ask your staff for their inputs on how to do things better. Even more important, you are going to have to **take action** when they provide their inputs.

In order to allow innovation to occur, you need to allow workers to **make time for it**. This may take time from other IT projects, but it will be well worth it. Once they've shared their ideas with you, it becomes your job to the hard work: executing on their ideas.

CIOs who learn how to collect innovative ideas and then turn them into IT department improvements **will have found the secret** to running a successful IT department. Nobody ever said that this was going to be easy. However, learn to do it right and some of that Steve Jobs magic just might show up in your IT department.

Chapter 11

---

3 Steps CIOs Can Take To Make Innovation Happen For Their IT Department

Chapter 11: 3 Steps CIOs Can Take To Make Innovation Happen For Their IT Department

"Be more innovative" – how many times has your CEO told you that? Although being innovative isn't really part of the definition of information technology, CIOs still want their IT department to always be **ahead of what their internal customers want**.

We'd like to be able to have our IT staff be solving problems that our customers might not even know that they have. However, it turns out that in the IT sector, being innovative is very hard to do. Good news – I've got three ways that a CIO can capture some of that innovation stuff and apply it to their IT department.

Ignite The Entrepreneur Spirit

Making innovation happen within an IT department is all about getting the individual members of the department to start to think in different ways. What can get overlooked all too often by CIOs is that this kind of thinking requires time.

In order to allow innovative thinking to occur, you need to free up your IT department to spend time thinking in innovative ways. Lots of companies such as Google and 3M have formalized programs to do this. They allocate a percentage of their staff's time (ranging from 15% to 20%) to work on project of their own choosing.

You may not be able to let your IT department free up that much of their time; however, any time that you can allow them to use to work on projects of their own choosing can only help to drive innovation. Simply showing your commitment to allowing them to be innovative will sometimes be enough to light the spark of innovation.

It's All About Words

Just exactly where does an innovation start? We'd like to think that it first shows up as a flash of insight in the mind of a solitary worker. However, more than often it really gets its start as the result of a conversation between two workers. Someone says something that gets the other person thinking and things take off from there.

As a CIO, you need to figure out a way to make sure that these types of conversations happen more often. One of the best sources for innovation causing conversations is when members of your IT department talk with people from different departments.

Depending on the size and the layout of your company, it can be difficult to set things up so that these types of conversations occur. However, thanks to online tools such as web sites and knowledge repositories, members of different departments can interact and share ideas.

You're Not Like Me

Finally, people who are similar to other people have very little to say to each other – they already know what the other person is thinking. As a CIO, you need to make sure that the IT department doesn't find itself in this kind of rut.

One way to make sure that this doesn't happen is to make sure that the people who are in the IT department are diverse. They may all look the same, but you want them to have different ways of looking at the world and different ways of thinking.

Reaching outside of the company to get in contact with teams that have different jobs or different outlooks can also help. Hospital emergency room teams have talked with racing team pit crews in order to better understand how more can be done in less time. Your IT department could probably talk with a team from another industry to gain similar insights.

What All Of This Means For You

Every CIO would like their IT department to be **more innovative** because it's a great way to show the importance of information technology, but exactly how to go about making this happen is something that too many of us struggle with. It turns out that it's not hard to do once you know how.

Three different ways to make innovation happen for your IT department include diving deep and really getting to know how your IT department's customers are using your services. You can build on this information and create probe projects that try out innovative new ideas with the expectation that most will fail, but all will produce good learning opportunities. Finally, you can tap into the power of your in-house staff: put their minds to work on how your IT department's products and services can be more innovative.

Everything is possible; the trick is in finding out **how to make it happen for your product**. Take the time to investigate these three suggestions and see if you can use them to add some innovation to your IT department's products and services in order to make them even more successful!

Chapter 12

CIO's Know That Finding The Right Way To Be Innovative Is The Hard Part

Chapter 12: CIO's Know That Finding The Right Way To Be Innovative Is The Hard Part

Among all of the other jobs that a modern CIO is expected to perform, there is also that pesky "pursue an innovation strategy" thing. This is so critical that it should almost be a part of the definition of information technology.

It's not that pushing the IT department to become more innovative is all that difficult, I mean anyone can do that. The hard part for a CIO is trying to pick and choose from all of the different ways to be innovative – **which way is the best for your IT department?**

It's All About Your People

Where does innovation come from? Can you go out to a store, buy it and then bring it back and distribute it among everyone who works in your IT department? **The answer is, of course, no.**

Instead, **innovation comes from within the people who work in your IT department**. This means that you need to make sure that you hire the right types of people.

Researchers Dr. Frank Tothaermel and Dr. Andrew Hess have looked into how IT departments can **boost their level of innovation**. What they found is that taking the time to focus on hiring and then cultivating the right types of people from the IT sector is what can make an IT department more innovative.

A very important point that they discovered is that not everyone in your IT department needs to be an innovator. Instead, **you actually need a mix of workers**. Some do need to be innovators – these are the IT employees who can create new ideas. The others don't need to be so innovative; however, they do need to be good at execution. They are the ones who will turn the innovative ideas into real products and services.

Do They Work Well Together?

Not all innovation in the IT department needs to come from within the department itself. Clever CIOs realize that they can boost the level of innovation by perusing both **alliances and acquisitions**.

What this means is that it can be worth a CIO's time to **form a joint venture** with another firm in order to investigate how their employees and services can make an IT department more innovative.

If it turns out that the joint venture provides enough value, then a CIO may want to **consider purchasing the firm** in order to boost IT innovation by permanently adding that firm's resources to the department.

This approach seems to work much better than the alternative of just finding a firm and buying it. Taking the time to see if the IT department and the other firm **are compatible** before making a purchase is always a good idea.

What All Of This Means For You

In order for your IT department to grow and prosper, you are going to need to be able to **find a way for it to become more innovative**. Your biggest challenge is going to be picking the right innovation strategy that will work with your department. This is a critical CIO skill because of the importance of information technology to the company.

There are no silver bullets available to make this happen. Instead, what you are going to have to do is to start by **hiring**

the right people into your IT department. This is going to have to be supplemented by having you take the time to pursue the correct alliances and acquisitions.

By combing both of these actions, you will be able to implement an innovation strategy that will work for both your IT department and your company. Once you've done this, you can sit back and **reap the benefits** of a successful innovation strategy.

It's from the forge of failure that the steel of success is formed.

Hard Work Does Not Guarantee Success, But Success Does Not Happen Without Hard Work.

- Dr. Jim Anderson

Create IT Departments That Are Productive And A Valuable Asset To The Rest Of The Company !

Dr. Jim Anderson is available to provide training and coaching on the topics that are the most important to people who have to manage IT departments: how can I build a productive IT department (and keep it together) while at the same time providing the rest of the company with the IT services that they need?

Dr. Anderson believes that in order to both learn and remember what he says, speakers need to laugh. Each one of his speeches is full of fun and humor so that what he says "sticks" with everyone.

Dr. Anderson's CIO SkillsTraining Includes:

4. How to identify and attract the right type of IT workers to your IT department.
5. How to build relationships with the company's senior management in order to get the support that you need?
6. How to stay on top of changing technology and security issues so that you never get surprised?

Dr. Jim Anderson works with over 100 customers per year. To invite Dr. Anderson to work with you, contact him at:

Phone: 813-418-6970 or
Email: jim@BlueElephantConsulting.com

Photo Credits:

Cover - By: Dennis Wilkinson
http://www.flickr.com/photos/djwtwo/

Chapter 1 - By: hellabella
http://www.flickr.com/photos/hel2005/

Chapter 2 - By: woodleywonderworks
http://www.flickr.com/photos/wwworks/

Chapter 3 - By: JD Lasica
http://www.flickr.com/photos/jdlasica/

Chapter 4 - By: Heating Oil
http://www.flickr.com/photos/heatingoil/

Chapter 5 - By: NikonFilm35
http://www.flickr.com/photos/nikonfilm35/

Chapter 6 - By: Gip Gipukan
http://www.flickr.com/photos/gipukan/

Chapter 7 - By: Friedemann Wulff-Woesten
http://www.flickr.com/photos/e2/

Chapter 8 - By: Sergio Alvarez
http://www.flickr.com/photos/tranchis/

Chapter 9 - By: Stefan
http://www.flickr.com/photos/dailyinvention/

Chapter 10 - By: Graham
http://www.flickr.com/photos/photograham/

Chapter 11 - By: Will Hastings
http://www.flickr.com/photos/willsan/

Chapter 12 - By: Willi Heidelbach
http://www.flickr.com/photos/wilhei/

Other Books By The Author

Product Management

- How To Have A Successful Product Manager Career: The Things That You Need To Be Doing TODAY In Order To Have A Successful Product Manager Career

- Product Manager Product Success: How to keep your product on track and make it become a success

- Communication Skills For Product Managers: The Communication Skills That Product Managers Need To Know How To Use In Order To Have A Successful Product

- Customer Lessons For Product Managers: Techniques For Product Managers To Better Understand What Their Customers Really Want

Public Speaking

- Secrets To Planning The Perfect Speech

- Secrets To Organizing The Perfect Speech: How to organize the best speech of your life!

- Secrets To Creating The Perfect Speech: How to create a speech that will make your message be remembered forever!

- How To Rehearse In Order To Give The Perfect Speech: How to effectively rehearse your next speech to that your message be remembered forever!

CIO Skills

- CIO Business Skills: How CIOs can work effectively with the rest of the company!

- Managing Your CIO Career: Steps That CIOs Have To Take In Order To Have A Long And Successful Career

- CIO Communication Skills Secrets: Tips And Techniques For CIOs To Use In Order To Become Better Communicators

IT Manager Skills

- IT Manager Budgeting Skills

- IT Manager Career Secrets: Tips And Techniques That IT Managers Can Use In Order To Have A Successful Career

Negotiating

- Preparing For Your Next Negotiation: What You Need To Do BEFORE A Negotiation Starts In Order To Get The Best Possible Deal

- How To Open Your Next Negotiation: How To Start A Negotiation In Order To Get The Best Possible Outcome

Miscellaneous

- Power Distribution Unit (PDU) Secrets: What Everyone Who Works In A Data Center Needs To Know!

- Making The Jump: How To Land Your Dream Job When You Get Out Of College!

Tips And Techniques For CIOs To Use In Order To Make Innovation Happen In Their IT Department

> This book has been written with one goal in mind – to show you how you bring the spirit of innovation into your IT department. It's not easy being a CIO so we're going to show you the strategies and techniques that you can use to introduce the spark of innovation in your IT department!
>
> **Let's Make Your CIO Career A Success!**

What You'll Find Inside:

- **CREATIVE ABRASION: HOW TO BUILD INNOVATION INTO IT**

- **FAUX MARKET SECRETS: HOW CIOS CAPTURE INNOVATION**

- **4 INNOVATION STRATEGIES THAT ACTUALLY WORK**

- **THE REASON THAT INNOVATION ISN'T HAPPENING IN YOUR IT DEPARTMENT**

Dr. Jim Anderson brings his 25 years of real-world experience to this book. He's been a senior IT executive at some of the world's largest firms. He's going to show you what you need to do (and not do!) in order to make your CIO career a success!

www.ingramcontent.com/pod-product-compliance
Lightning Source LLC
Chambersburg PA
CBHW071806170526
45167CB00003B/1199